DRAW OCEANIA

AN EASY STEP-BY-STEP APPROACH

BY
Kristin J. Draeger

Copyright 2017 by Kristin J. Draeger

All rights reserved. No part of this book may be reproduced, stored in a retrieval system, or transmitted in any form or by any means, electronic, mechanical, photocopying, recording, or otherwise, without the prior written permission of Kristin J. Draeger.

All of the maps in this book were drawn by Kristin J. Draeger and are copyrighted by Kristin J. Draeger ©2017. The majority of the tiny buildings on the cover and interior pages were drawn by Marina Zlochin ©2017.

ArtK12.com
info@artk12.com

Instructions

The Map

In this volume students learn to draw Polynesia, Micronesia, Melanesia, Australia, and the surrounding bodies of water. Because there are so many tiny islands in this area of the world, I have tried to make it simpler by first having the student draw outlines around groups of them in order to easily identify which islands belong to which country or territory. To make them easier to remember I have tried to make each outline look like an ocean creature.

The Drawing

For this drawing use a plain 8 1/2 x 11 or an 11 x 14.25 (trimmed from an 11 x 17 ledger-sized paper) turned horizontally. Follow the instructions in red, page by page, until the end of the book is reached, labeling the countries as you go. It is helpful for the student, when drawing each step, to ask "Where does the line begin?" and "Where does it end?" It is also helpful to mark these beginnings and endings with a dot before drawing the line.

The map can be drawn all at once, but students may find it easier to master smaller portions of the map at a time. After drawing a portion of the map students may want to pause and practice what they have learned.

Coloring

If the student wishes to color the map, I recommend first inking it with a thin, black, permanent marker. This will help maintain the integrity of the outline and give the final product a more "professional" look.

Enjoy.

For Lucy Conway, who loves the ocean.
Thank you for all your help.

PAPER

Before you begin to draw your map of Oceania you will need to prepare your paper. If you are using a ledger-sized piece of paper, trim it to 11 x 14 1/4 inches. If you are using an 8 1/2 x 11 sheet of paper you are ready to go! Regardless of what sized paper you are using, begin by folding it into quarters. The dotted lines are the fold lines.

POLYNESIA

Oceania can be divided into three cultural areas: Polynesia, Melanesia and Micronesia. The islands within these three groups are populated by these three different cultural groups. We will begin by drawing what is called the Polynesian Triangle. Place three dots as shown.

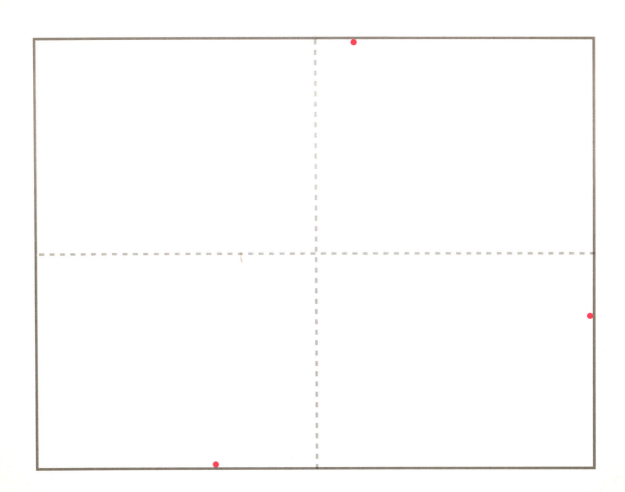

POLYNESIA

Connect the dots. Indigenous people that live on islands within this section of the Pacific Ocean are Polynesian.

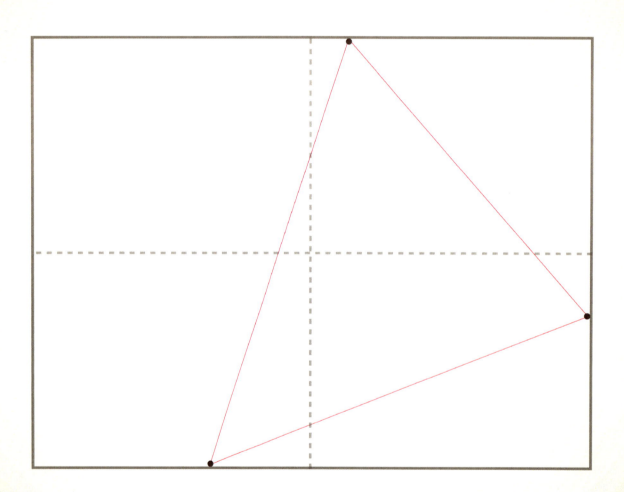

POLYNESIA

Add these three dots.

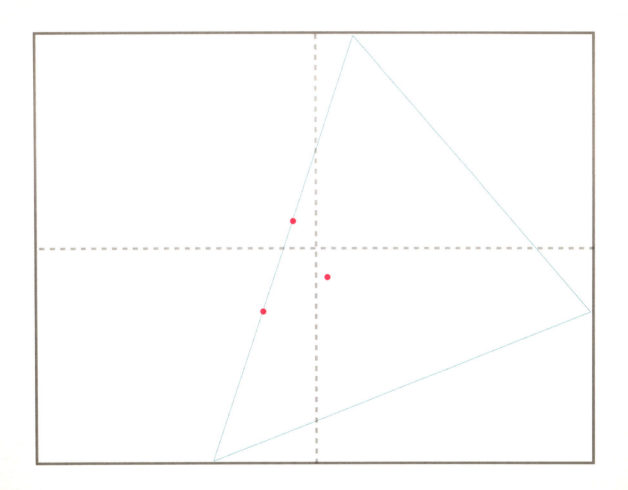

MELANESIA

Now connect the dots as shown and erase the dotted line. This area of the Polynesian Triangle belongs to the next section which is called Melanesia.

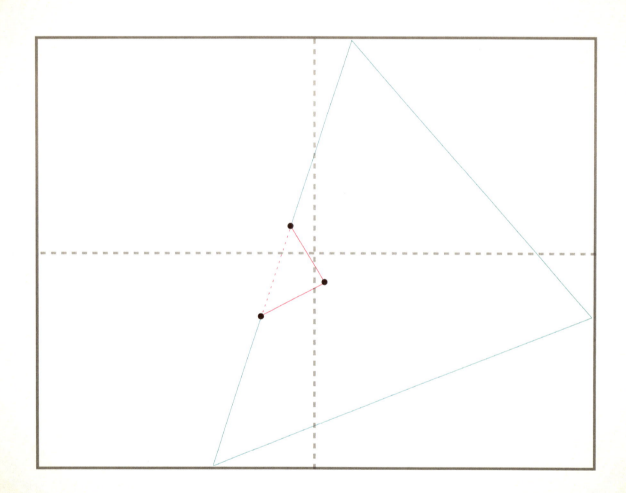

MELANESIA

Add two more dots.

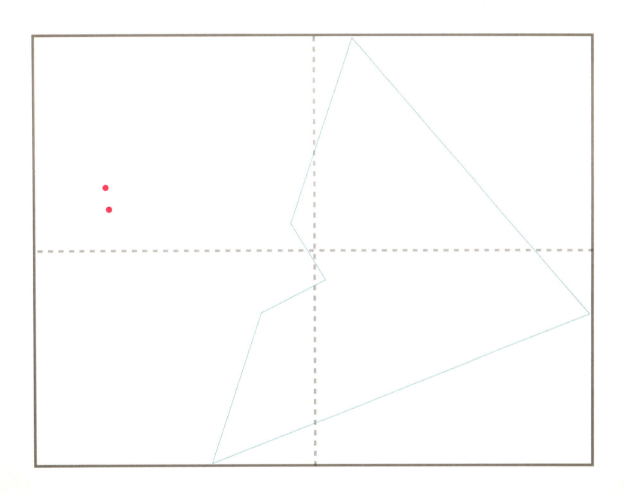

MELANESIA

Indigenous people that live on islands within this section of the Pacific Ocean belong to the Melanesian culture.

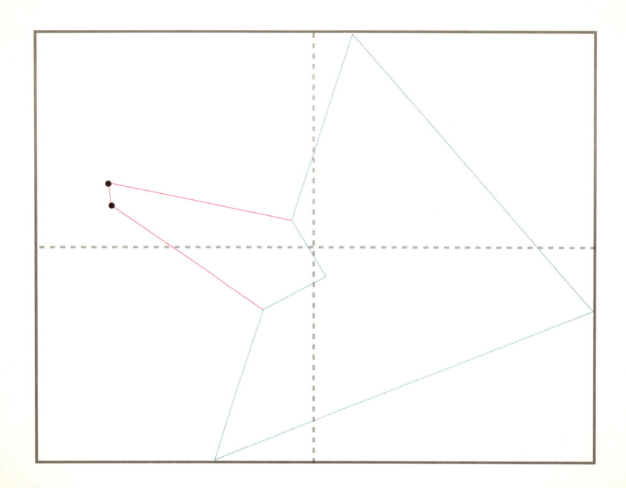

12

Add two more dots.

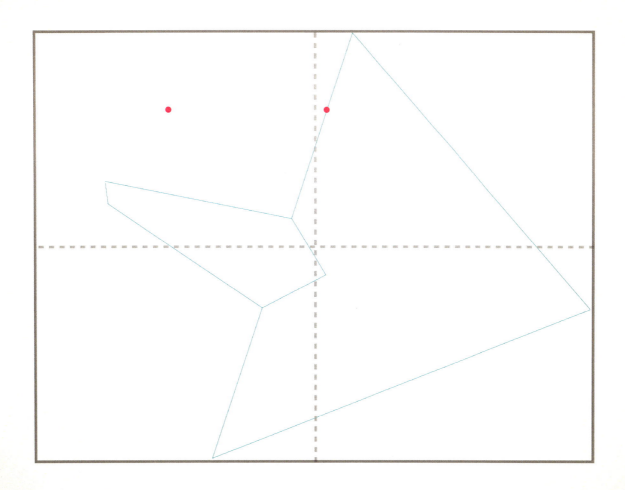

MICRONESIA

This section of the Pacific Ocean is called Micronesia and its indigenous inhabitants belong to the Micronesian culture.

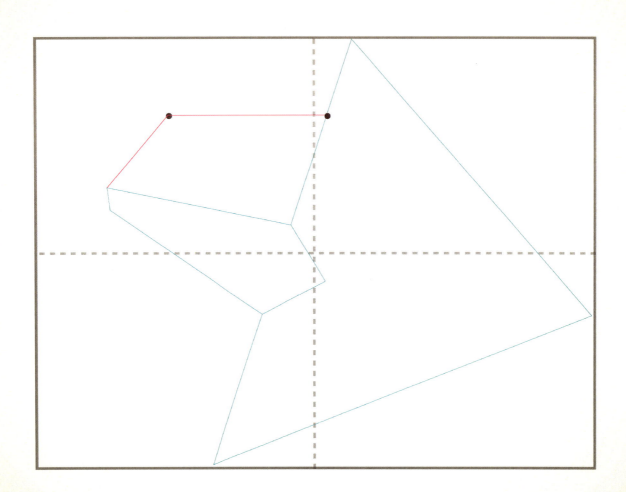

HAWAII

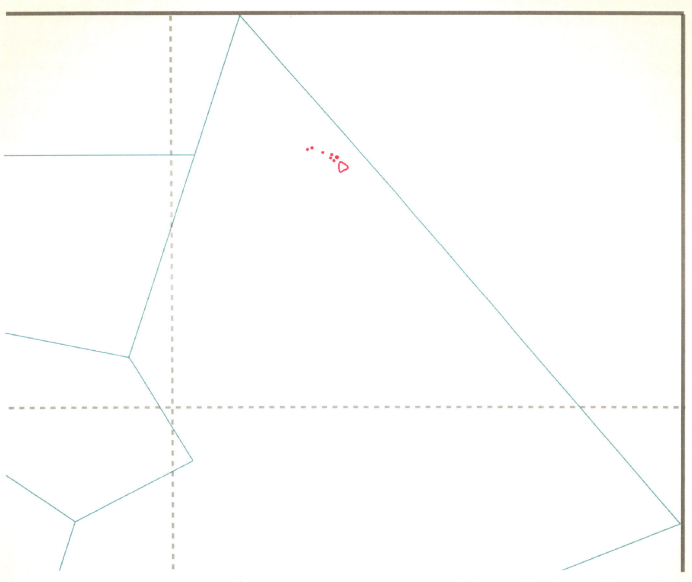

Keeping your paper horizontal, we are now going to concentrate on the top right section. At the top of the Polynesian Triangle is the state of Hawaii. Hawaii contains two groups of islands*: first draw the eight main islands.

*In this book we will refer to the variety of "islands" in the South Pacific (coral islands, cays, keys and atolls) as simply islands, otherwise it would become very complicated

HAWAII

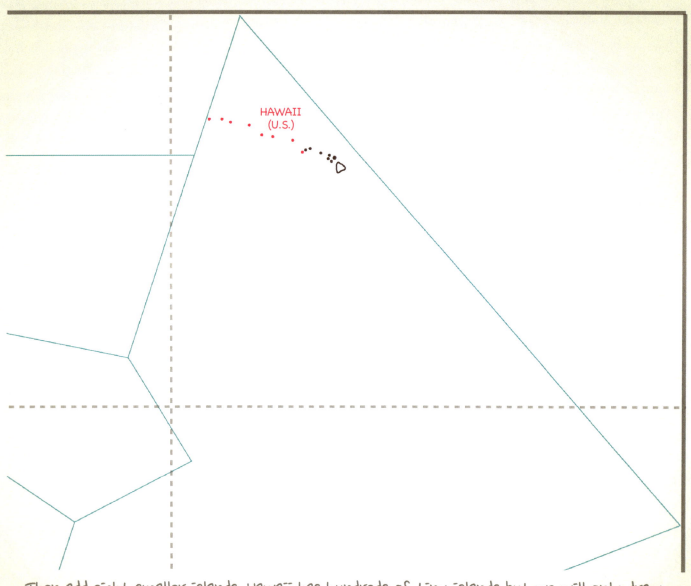

Then add eight smaller islands. Hawaii has hundreds of tiny islands but we will only draw sixteen. Hawaii is a member of the United States.

NEW ZEALAND

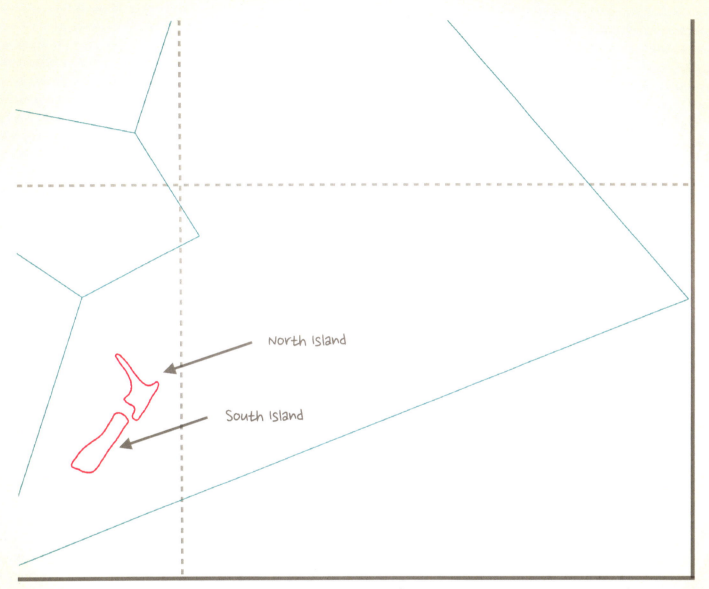

The country of New Zealand lies at the bottom of the Polynesian Triangle. Begin by drawing the two largest islands: North Island and South Island.

NEW ZEALAND

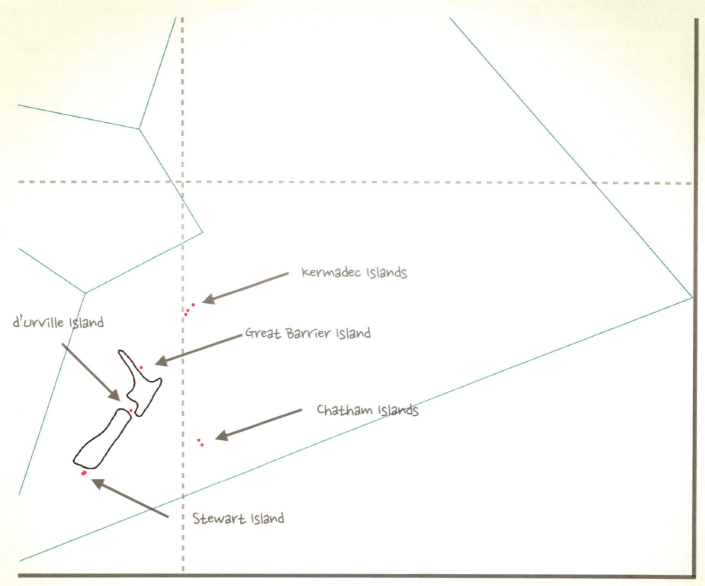

New Zealand contains many islands. Here are some of the larger ones: Stewart Island, the Chatham Islands, Great Barrier Island, d'Urville Island, the Bounty Islands, and the Kermadec Islands.

NEW ZEALAND

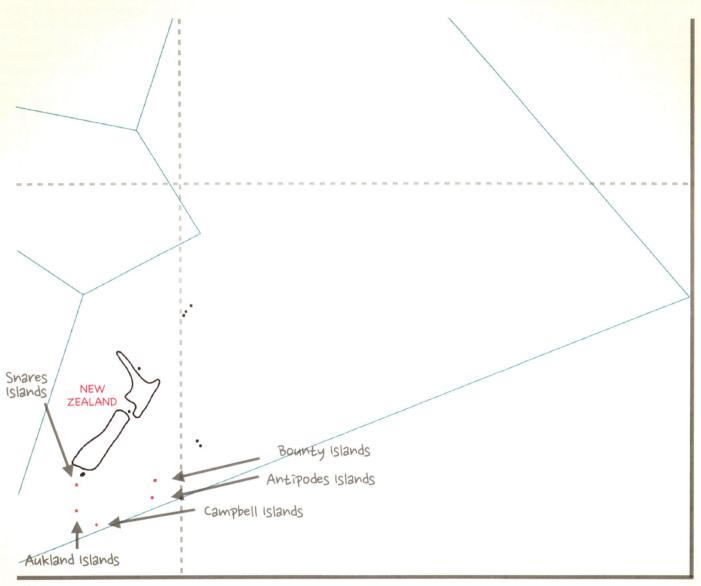

Below the two main islands are five more groups of islands*: The Snares, Aukland, Campbell, Antipodes and the Bounty Islands.

*Many of the islands in this book are so small we will sometimes represent entire groups of them with just one dot.

EASTER ISLAND

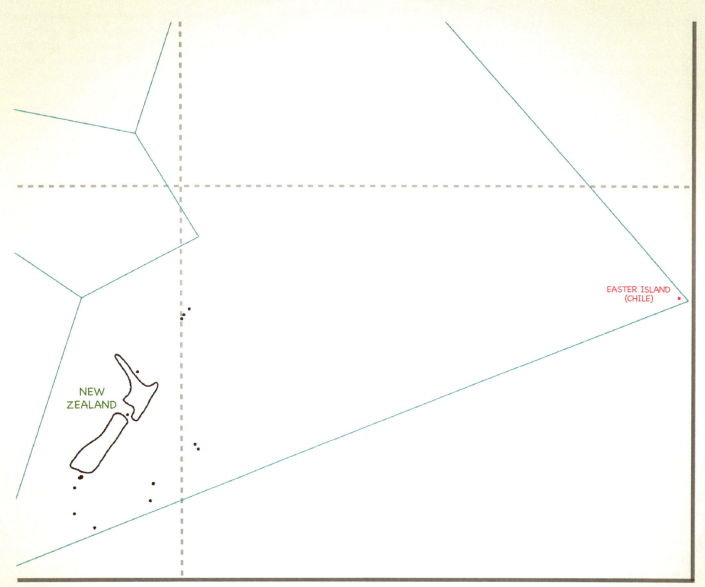

The third and easternmost point of the Polynesian Triangle is Easter Island. Easter Island is a tiny island that is a territory of Chile.

KIRIBATI

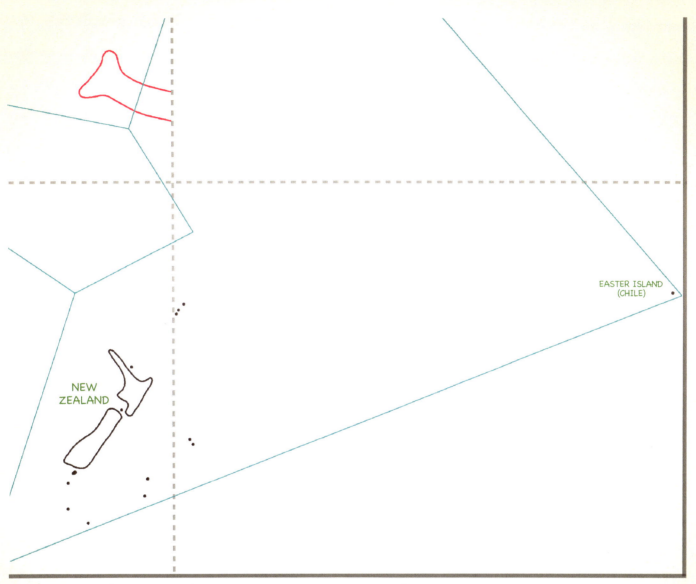

The rest of the islands in Oceania are so tiny and numerous that we are going to draw outlines around them so that we can tell which islands belong to which country. To make them easier to remember we will make each outline look like an ocean creature. The outline of the country of Kiribati looks like a Hammerhead Shark. Here is its tail. Notice that part of it is in Micronesia.

KIRIBATI

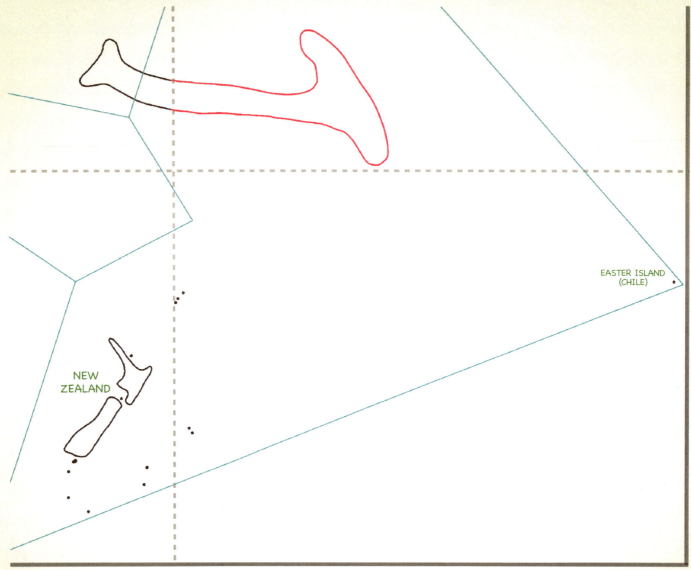

Here is the front of the Hammerhead Shark (it is a very simple shark), or as we will call it, the Kiribammerhead Shark.

KIRIBATI

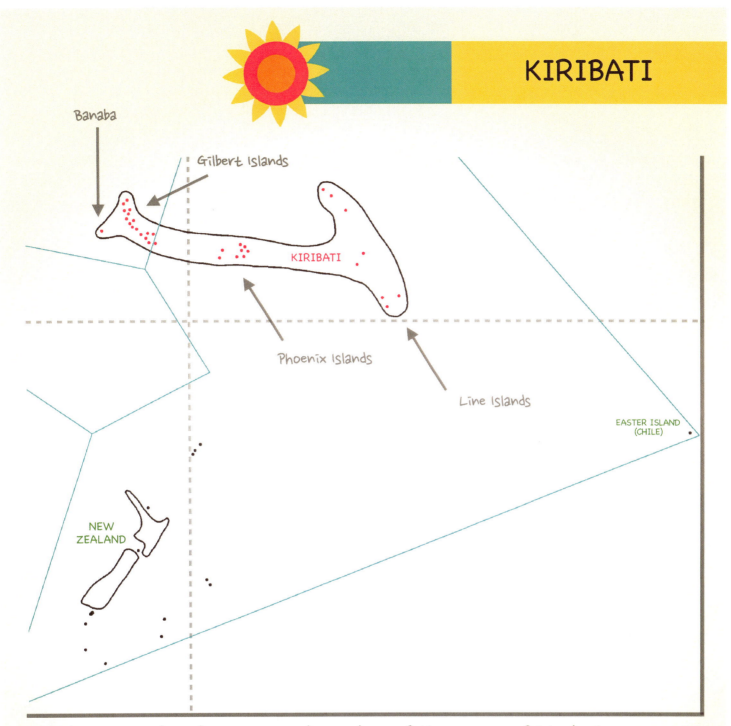

Kiribati is an independent nation and is made up of three groups of islands plus one single island. The single island, Banaba, is in the tail. The group of sixteen islands in the tail are called the Gilbert Islands. The eight islands in the shark's belly are called the Phoenix Islands and the eight* islands across his head are called the Line Islands.

*The Line Islands actually contain 11 islands, but only 8 belong to Kiribati; we will draw the other three later.

COOK ISLANDS

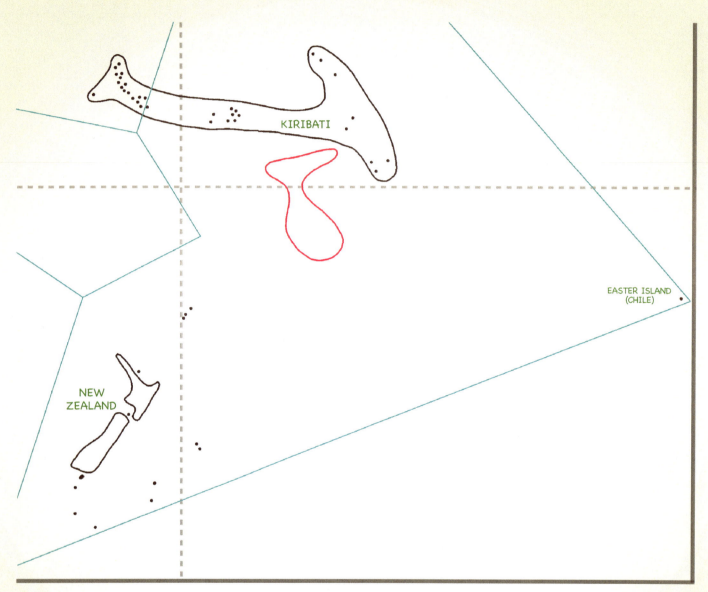

The next group of islands that we will outline are the Cook Islands. Their outline looks a bit like a goldfish or maybe even a fish cracker. We will call it the Cook Cracker.

COOK ISLANDS

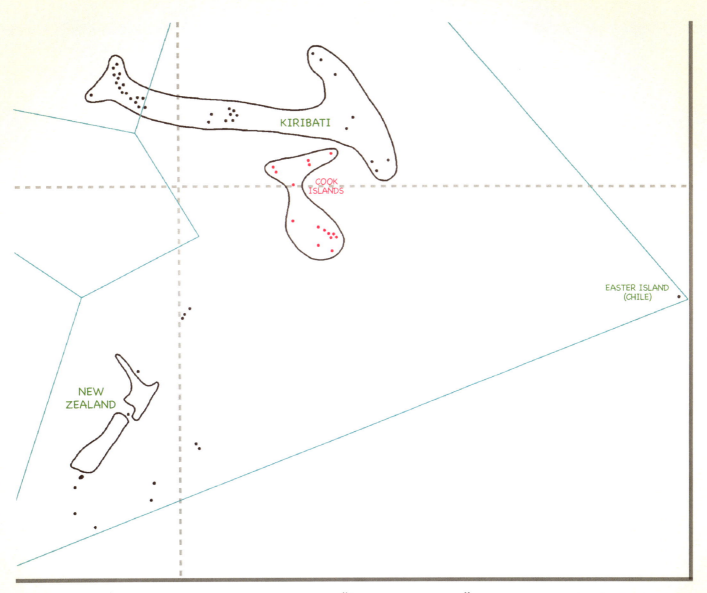

Cook Island is a self-governing country in "free-association" with New Zealand.* It contains fifteen islands and two submerged reefs (which we will not draw).

*Free association is a technical term that means that they are independent, but have partnered with a larger country for certain needs. It's complicated.

FRENCH POLYNESIA

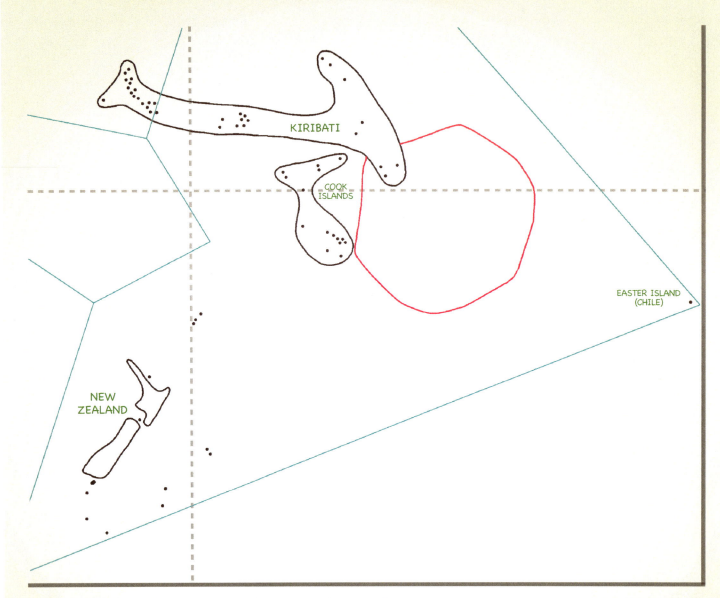

South of the Kiribammerhead shark and east of the Cook Cracker is a Stingray. The body of the Stingray contains the islands of French Polynesia.

FRENCH POLYNESIA

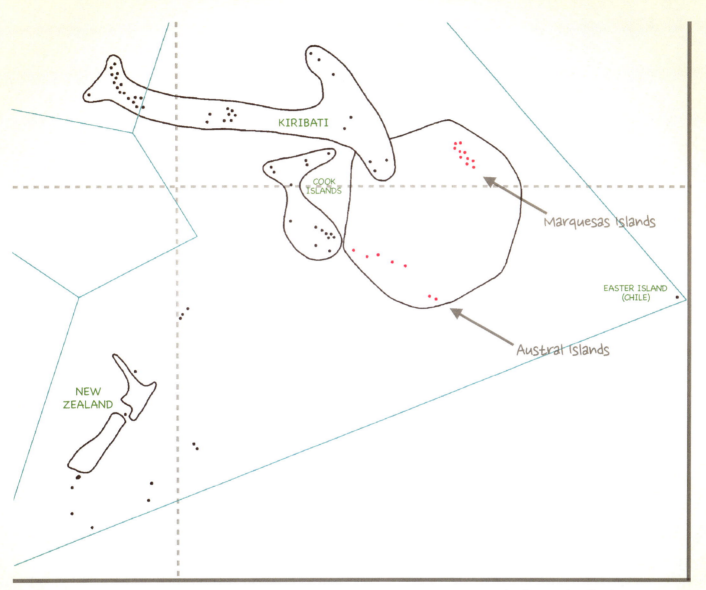

French Polynesia is a French overseas collectivity.* It is composed of 118 islands (we will not draw them all) in five groups. On the ray's left flank is a long group of seven islands called the Austral Islands. On his right flank is a tighter group of islands called the Marquesas Islands, of which we will draw the ten main islands.

*An overseas collectivity, as a territory of France, has representation in the French Parliament; its citizens have French nationality and they vote for the President of France. The overseas collectivity also has some autonomy. It's complicated.

FRENCH POLYNESIA

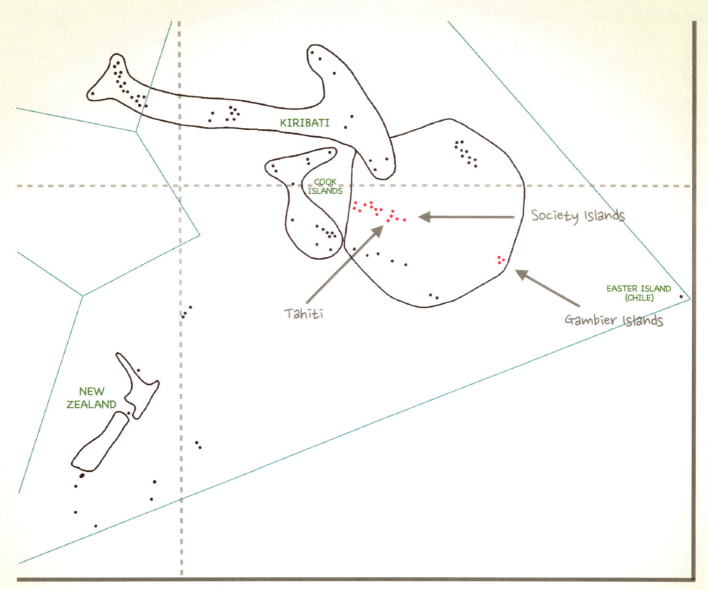

North of the Austral Islands are the eleven Society Islands. Among these is the well-known island of Tahiti. And at the back of the stingray, where the tail will connect is a small group of fourteen islands called the Gambier Islands (we will draw the three largest*).

*The Gambier Islands are so tiny and so close together that we couldn't possibly draw them all while maintaining proper proportions.

FRENCH POLYNESIA

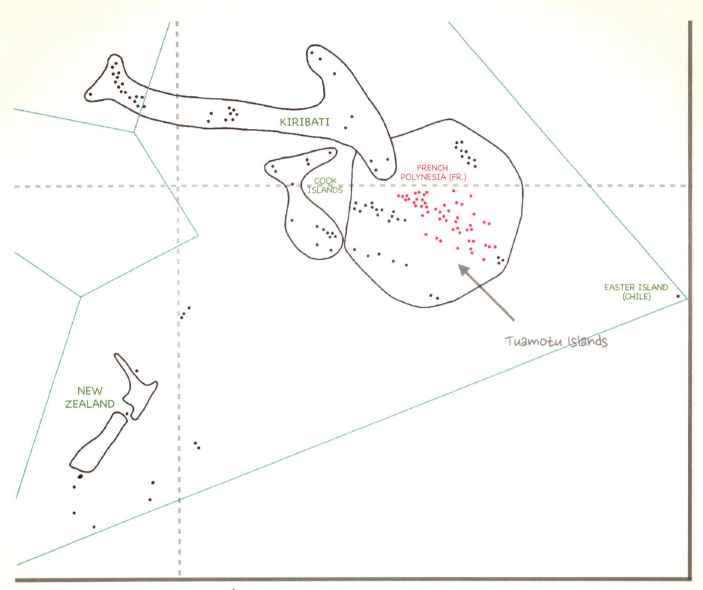

Tuamotu Islands

Down the middle of the ray's back is the fifth and largest group of islands called the Tuamotu Islands. Technically there are 78 islands in the group, but again we have only drawn about 50 of the largest. (Just think of it as practice for dotting i's.)

PITCAIRN ISLANDS

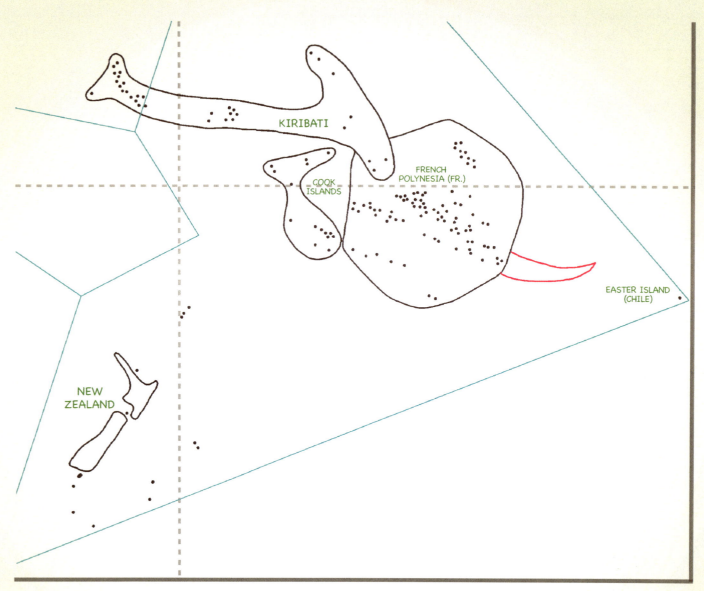

The Stingray has a tail that extends about half way toward Easter Island.

PITCAIRN ISLANDS

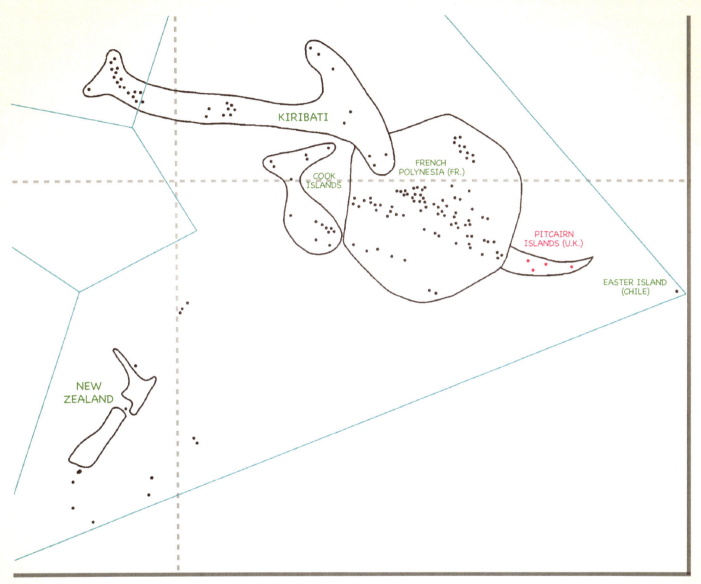

In the tail are four islands called the Pitcairn Islands. These islands are a British territory.

TONGA

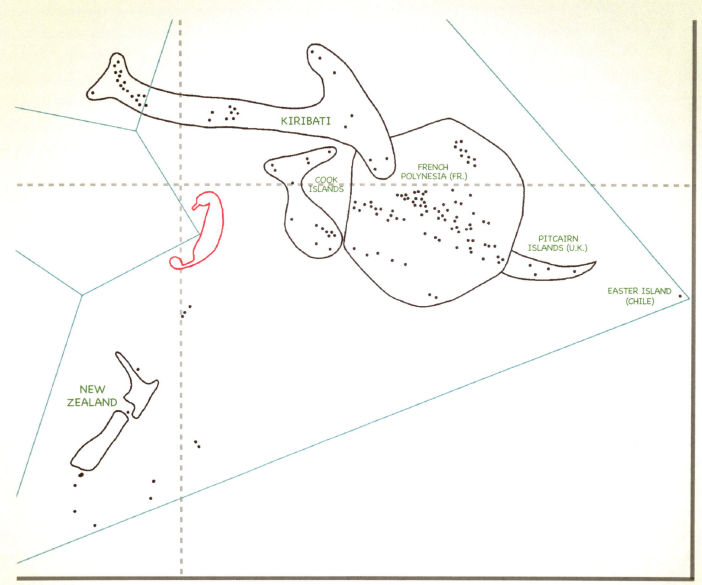

On the eastern edge of the Polynesian Triangle, with his belly up against Melanesia is the island country of Tonga. The islands of Tonga fit nicely into the outline of a seahorse; we will call him the Tongahorse.

TONGA

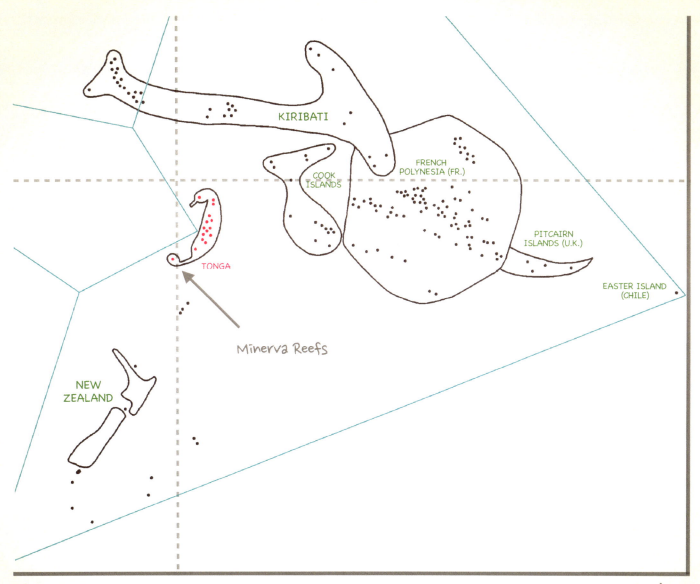

Minerva Reefs

Tonga has 169 islands! We will only draw fourteen of the larger ones. In the Tongahorse's tail is a group of two uninhabited reefs called the Minerva Reefs.

TUVALU

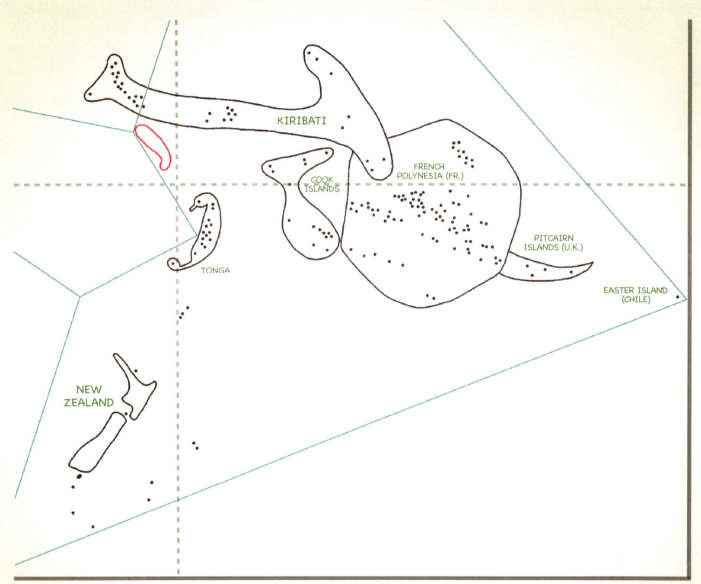

Tucked up under the Kiribammerhead shark is a sea slug* which outlines the independent island country of Tuvalu, or as we will call it, the Tuvalug.

*A sea slug is the common name for a sea snail without a shell, or a nudibranch, or sometimes called a short sea cucumber.

TUVALU

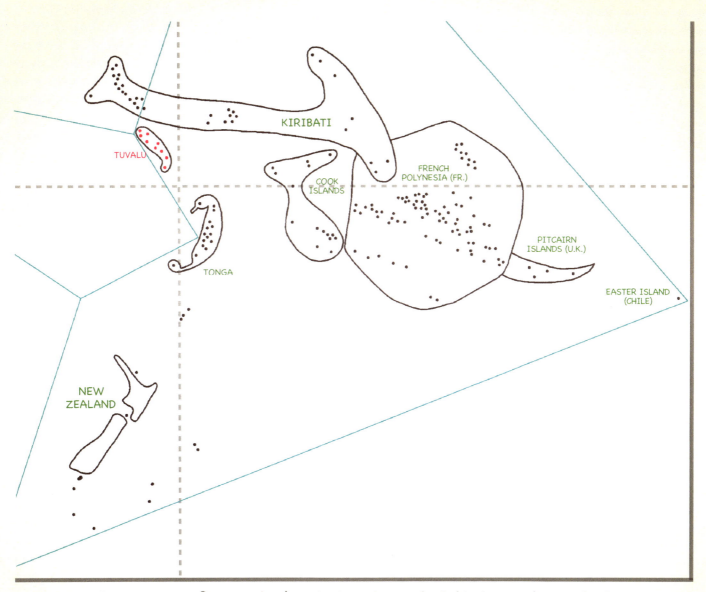

The Tuvalug consists of nine islands, which makes it look like a sea slug with the chicken pox.

AMERICAN SAMOA

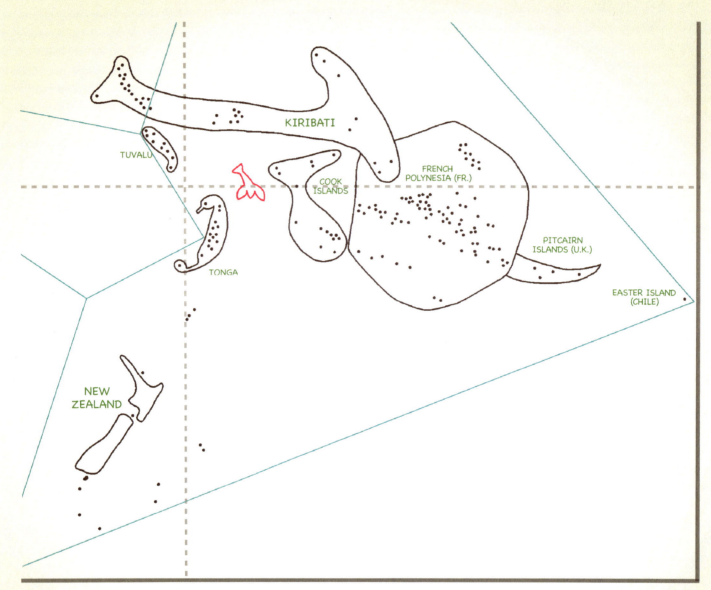

American Samoa, a territory of the US, is a tiny lobster between the Cook Cracker and the Tongahorse. Maybe we could call it the American Samobster.

AMERICAN SAMOA

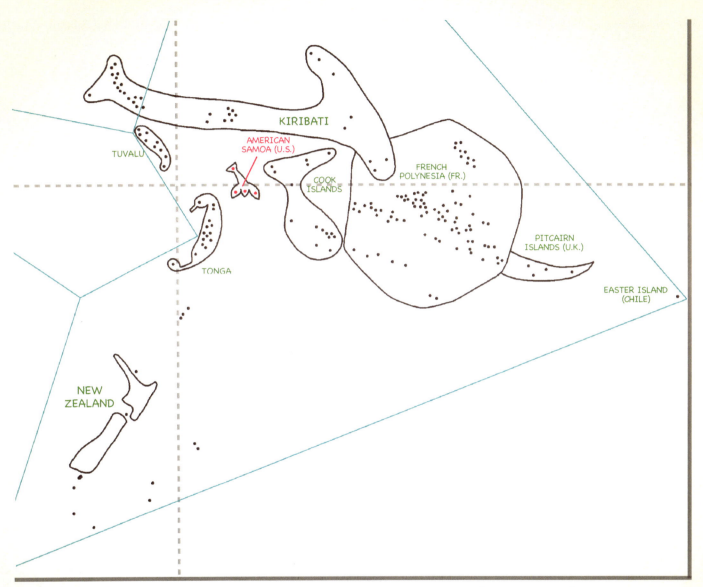

American Samoa, I mean, the American Samobster, consists of seven islands. We will draw only four of the islands because the two on the Samobster's head are so close together we have to represent them with one dot.

WALLIS & FUTUNA

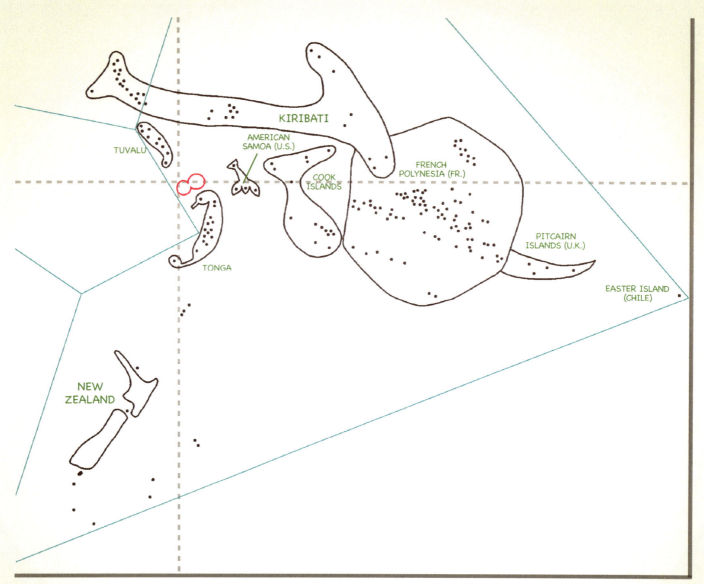

Deep down in the ocean below the Tongahorse and the Tuvalug is a Bigeye Tuna.* He is so deep in the ocean you can only see his two beady eyes. First draw the outline of his eyeballs.

*Yup, there is really a species of tuna called this and they really do have big eyes.

WALLIS & FUTUNA

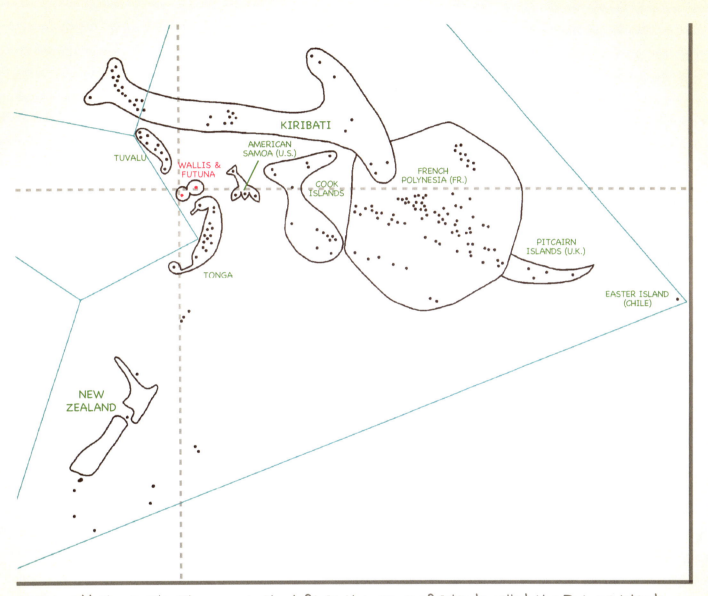

Now add the pupils. The eye on the left is the group of islands called the Futuna Islands (sometimes called the Hoon Islands), and the eye on the right is the group of islands called the Wallis Islands. This French overseas collectivity is called Wallis and Futuna, or as we will call it, Wallis The Tuna.

NIUE, SAMOA & TOKELAU

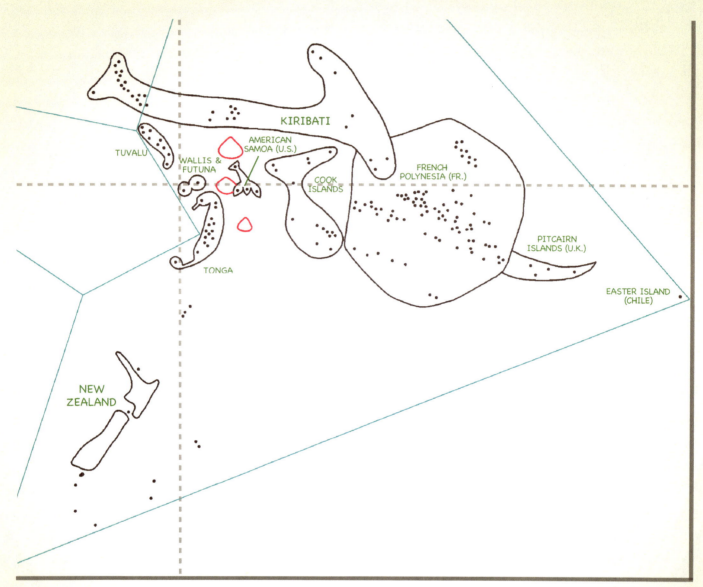

Below the belly of the Kiribammerhead Shark are three clams.

 # NIUE, SAMOA & TOKELAU

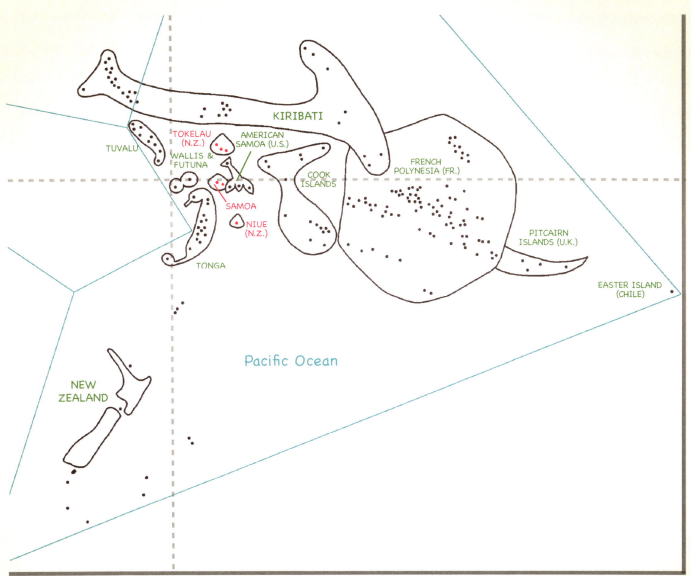

The top clam has three pearls; the middle clam has two pearls and the bottom clam has one pearl. The top clam is Tokelau, a territory of New Zealand, which is made up of three islands. The middle clam is the independent country of Samoa which has two main islands and the bottom clam is the independent country of Niue which consists of a single island.

MICRONESIA & PALAU

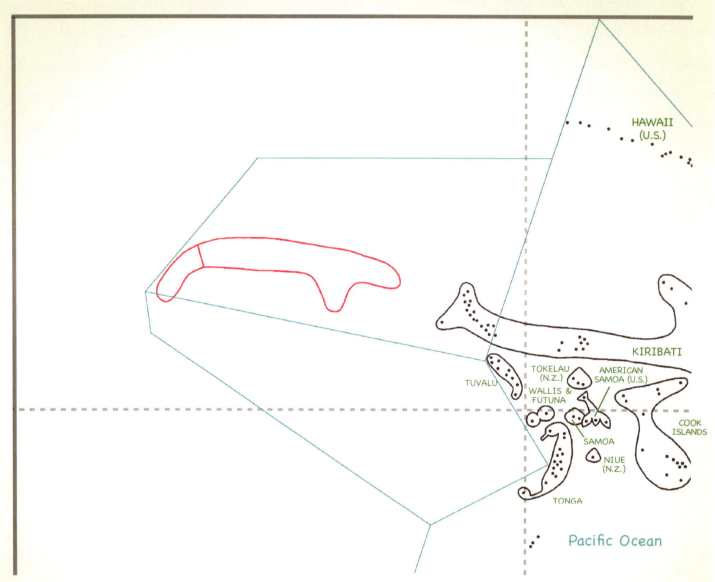

We are now basically finished with the Polynesian Triangle and will move on to Micronesia. The star of Micronesia is the Moray Eel. This outline will contain the Caroline Island archipelago which is divided among two independent countries: Micronesia* and Palau.

*This is a bit confusing. Micronesia is the name of the area AND the name of a country in that area. Technically the country is called the Federated States of Micronesia, but is usually referred to as simply Micronesia.

MICRONESIA & PALAU

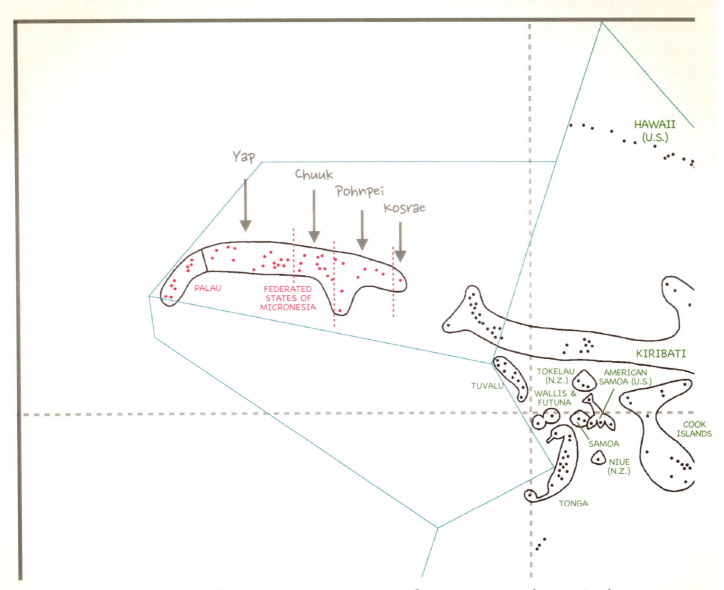

The islands in the body of the eel are the country of Micronesia, and the islands in the tail belong to the country of Palau. We will refer to the whole eel as the Federated-States-of-the-Micronesian-Eel-and-His-Tail-Which-Is-a-Separate-Country-called-Palau. Got it? Micronesia contains four states: Yap, Chuuk, Pohnpei and Kosrae.*

*You do not have to draw the dotted lines.

43

NORTHERN MARIANA ISLANDS & GUAM

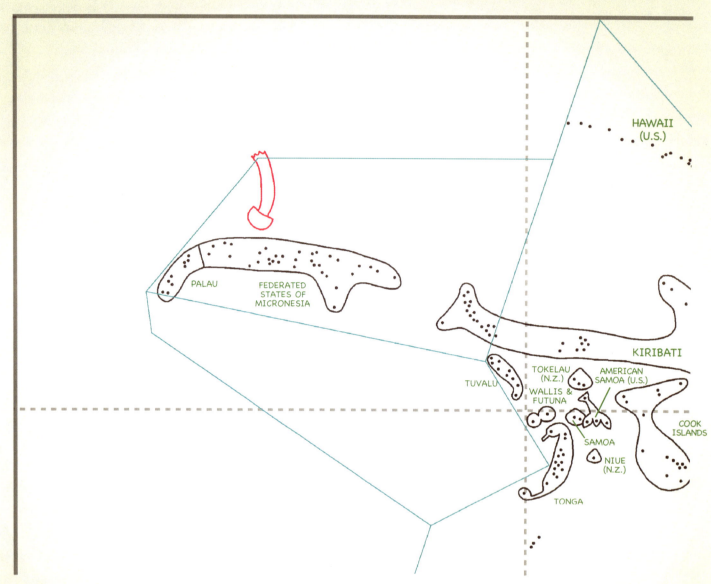

Above the Federated-States-of-the-Micronesian-Eel-and-His-Tail-Which-Is-a-Separate-Country-called-Palau is an upside-down jellyfish. This creature will contain the Mariana Islands which are politically split into two distinct groups: Guam and the Northern Mariana Islands.

NORTHERN MARIANA ISLANDS & GUAM

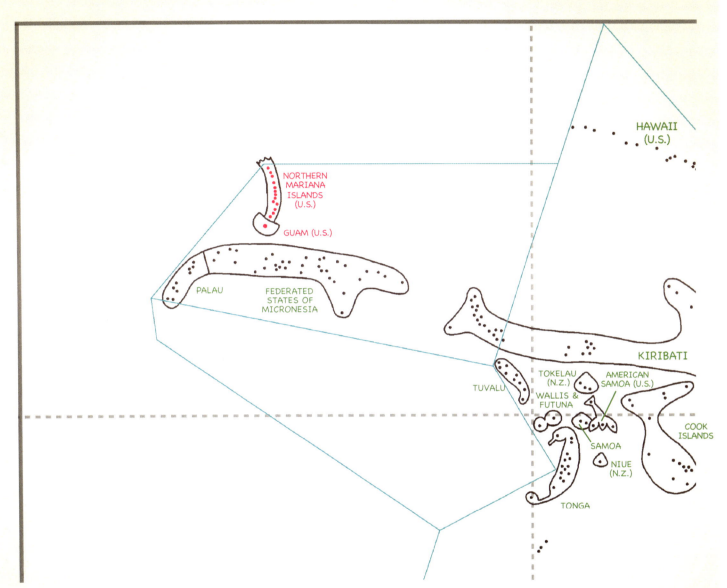

The head of the jellyfish contains the single island of Guam, a territory of the US. The tentacle thingy contains the Northern Mariana Islands, a group of fourteen islands, which is a commonwealth* of the US.

*There is very little difference between a commonwealth and a territory. In fact, a commonwealth is just a specific type of territory. Again, it's complicated.

MARSHALL ISLANDS

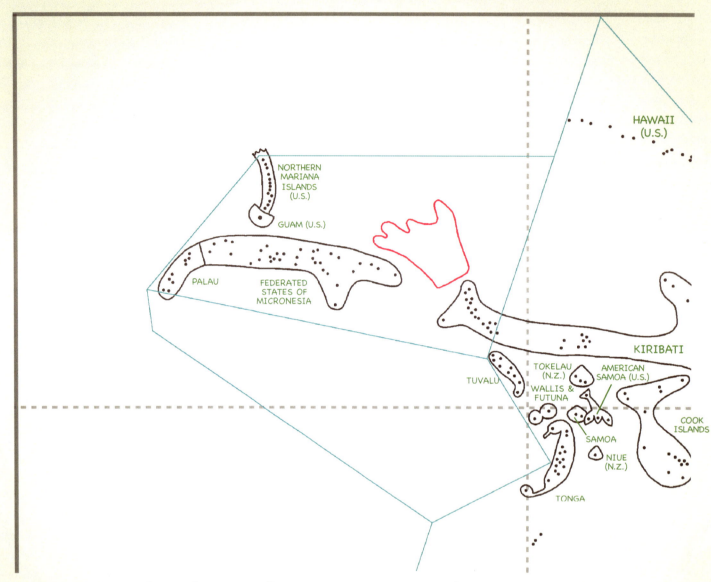

Between the Federated-States-of-the-Micronesian-Eel-and-His-Tail-Which-Is-a-Separate-Country-called-Palau and the tail of the Kiribammerhead shark is a blob of coral. This coral outlines the Marshall Islands that are an independent country in "free association" with the United States.

MARSHALL ISLANDS

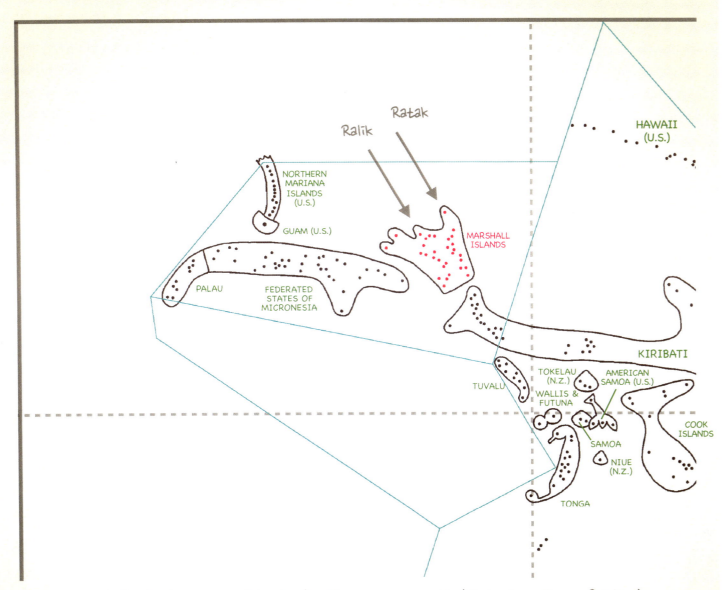

The Marshall Islands contain 34 islands. These are separated into two lines of islands: the Ratak* group on the east and the Ralik* group on the west.

*Ratak means "sunrise" (which is why they are on the east side), and Ralik means "sunset" (which is why they are on the west side).

NAURU

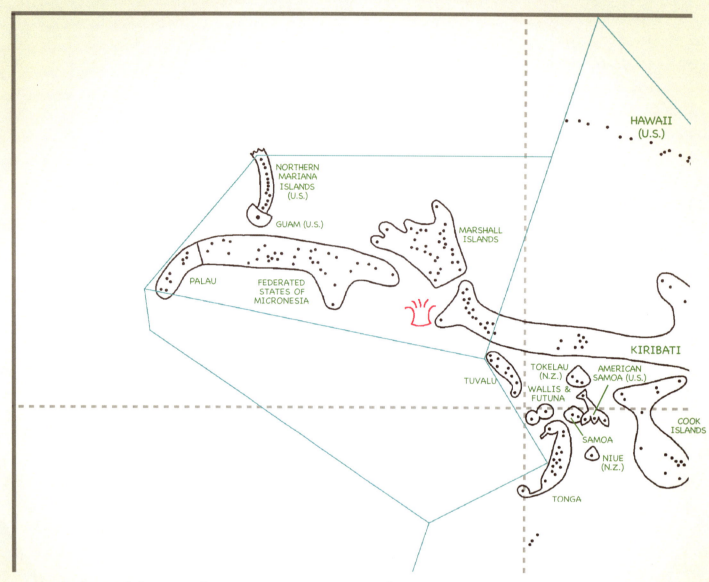

The Federated-States-of-the-Micronesian-Eel-and-His-Tail-Which-Is-a-Separate-Country-called-Palau is about to eat the small island of Nauru. We will represent Nauru as an anemone which we will call the Anemonauru.

NAURU

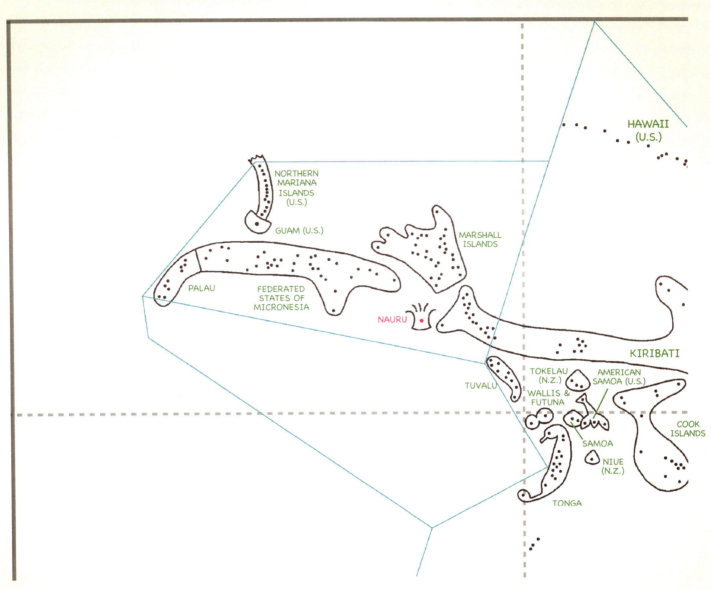

The Anemonauru is a single, tiny independent island country (only eight square miles). So far, the Federated-States-of-the-Micronesian-Eel-and-His-Tail-Which-Is-a-Separate-Country-called-Palau has not gobbled it up.

US TERRITORIES

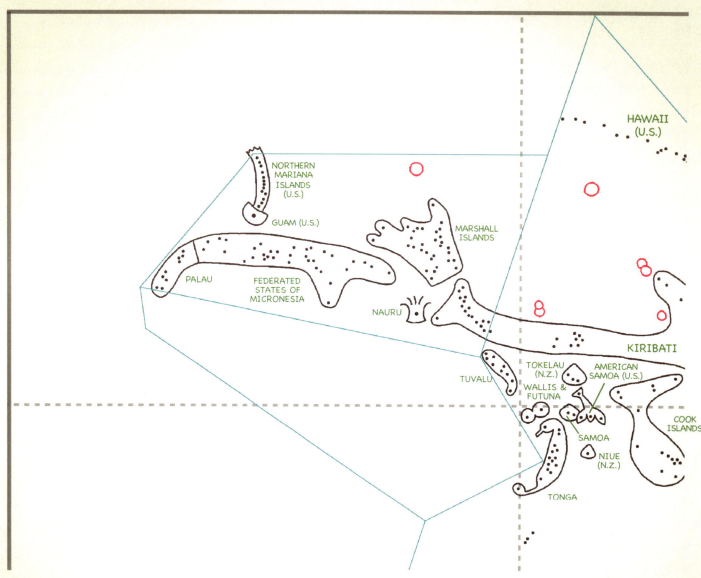

Finally, we will add seven US island territories to the area (one in Micronesia and six in Polynesia). We will represent them as sand dollars. They all belong to the US and all seven are uninhabited.

US TERRITORIES

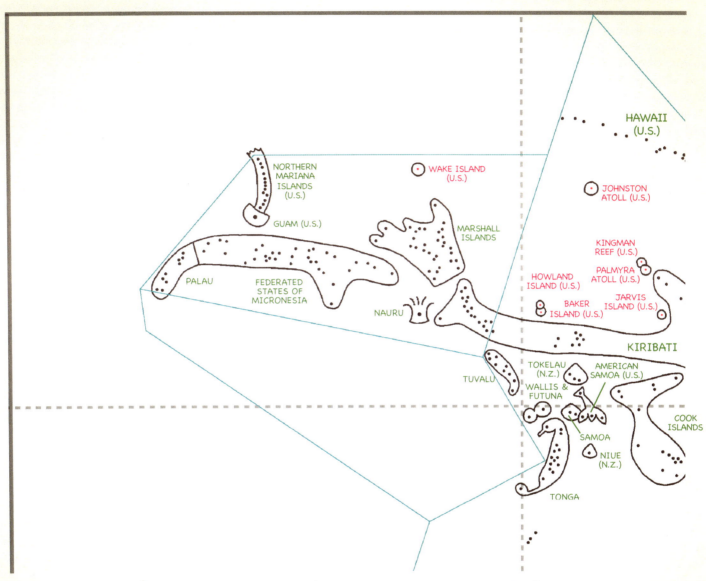

The sand dollars' names are: Wake Island, Johnston Atoll, Kingman Reef, Palmyra Atoll, Jarvis, Howland and Baker Islands.

SOLOMON ISLANDS

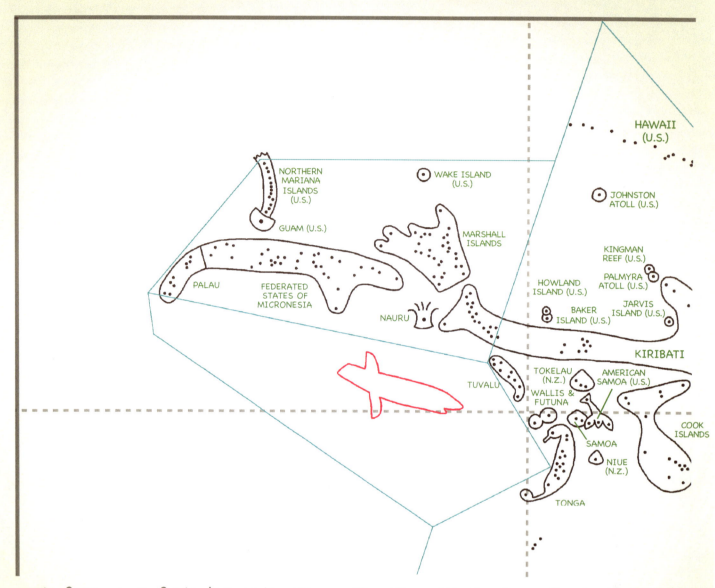

The first group of islands in Melanesia we will outline with the shape of a shark that has no tail.

# SOLOMON ISLANDS

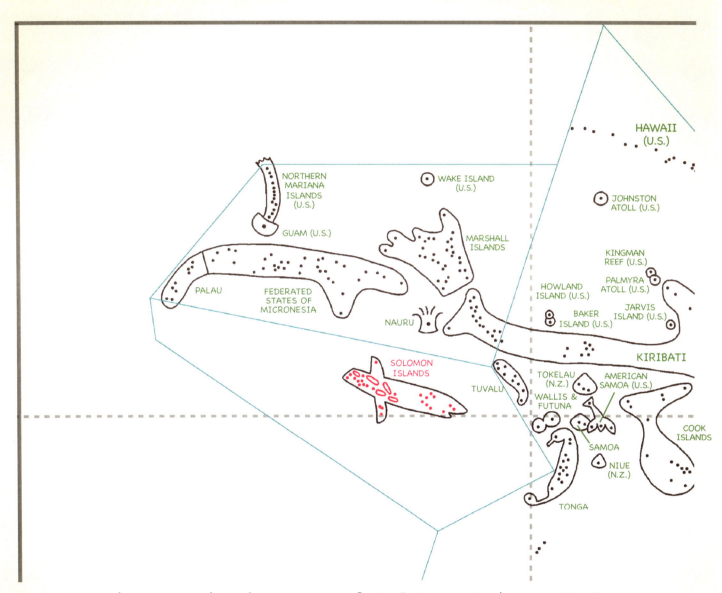

These islands are the independent country of the Solomon Islands. We will call them the Sharkomon Islands. This group contains more than 900 islands, but we will only draw the six large islands and a few smaller ones.

VANUATU

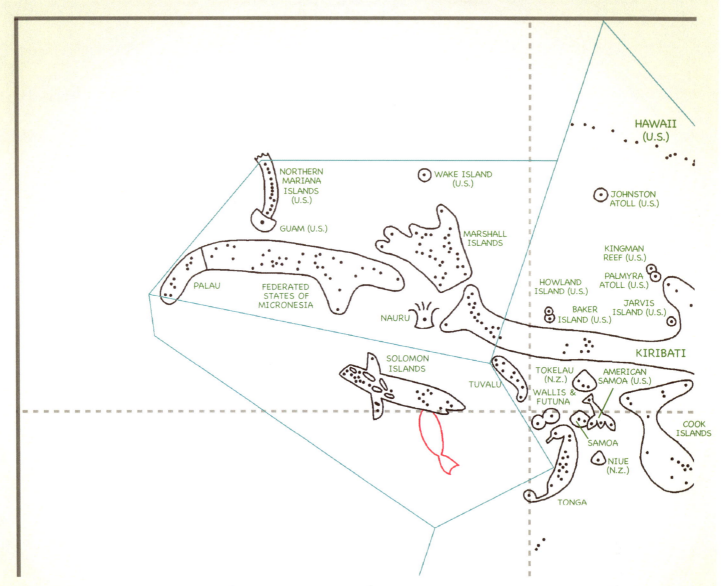

Below the Sharkomon Islands is another tuna fish. This one is a Little Tuna* and outlines the independent country of Vanuatu, which we will call the Vanuatuna. The Vanuatuna is a very bold little tunafish!

*Yup, there really is a species of tunafish called the Little Tuna.

VANUATU

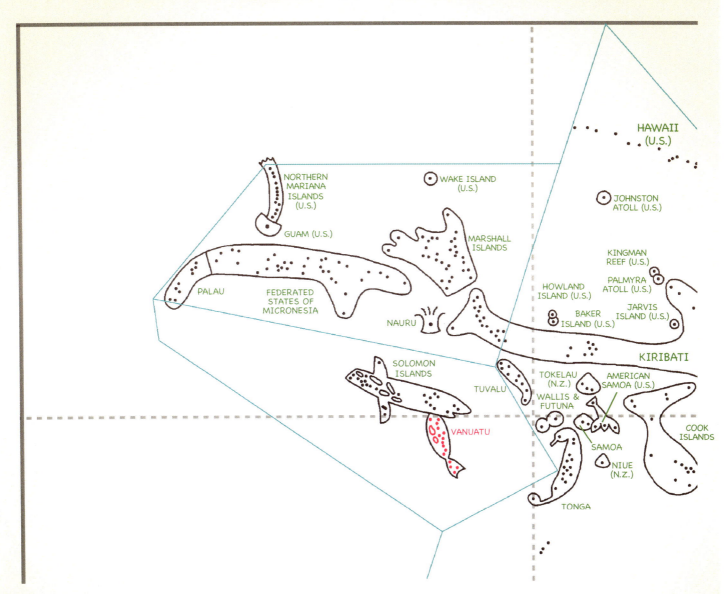

The Vanuatuna consists of 82 islands, but we will only draw seventeen of the largest.

FIJI

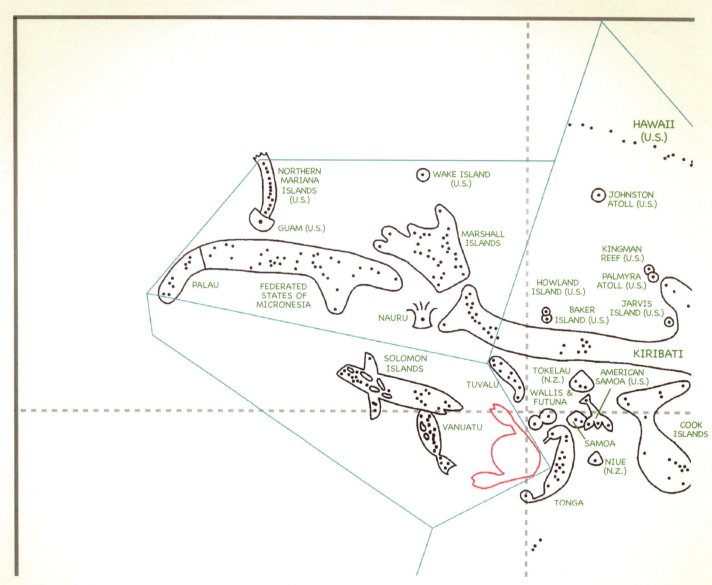

Backed up into the eastern corner of Melanesia is a crab which outlines the country of Fiji. This crab has his claws drawn protecting the Tongahorse from the Sharkomon Islands. (The Tuvalug has turned his head to watch, and Wallis The Tuna looks nervous.)

FIJI

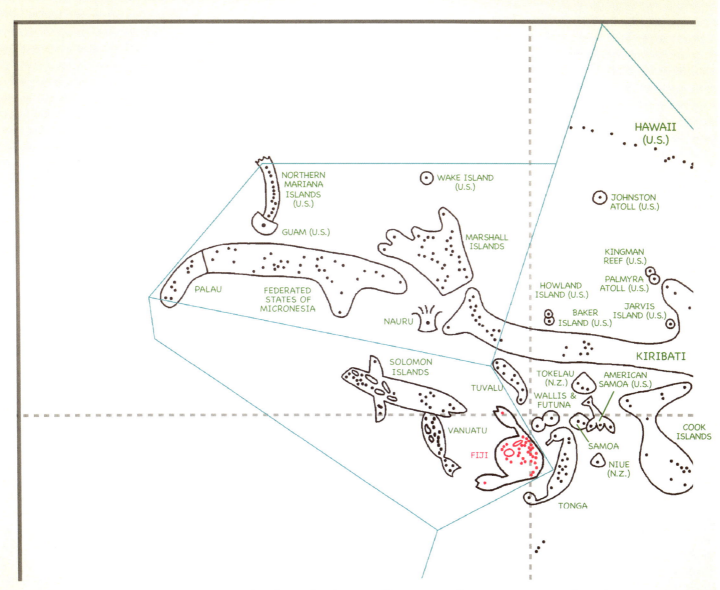

Fiji contains more than 830 islands and islets,* about 100 of which are inhabited. Notice that there is one island in each of its claws. The largest island in the middle of its forehead is called Viti Levu.

*Tiny islands are called islets just like tiny pigs are called piglets. The only difference is that islets don't grow up.

NEW CALEDONIA

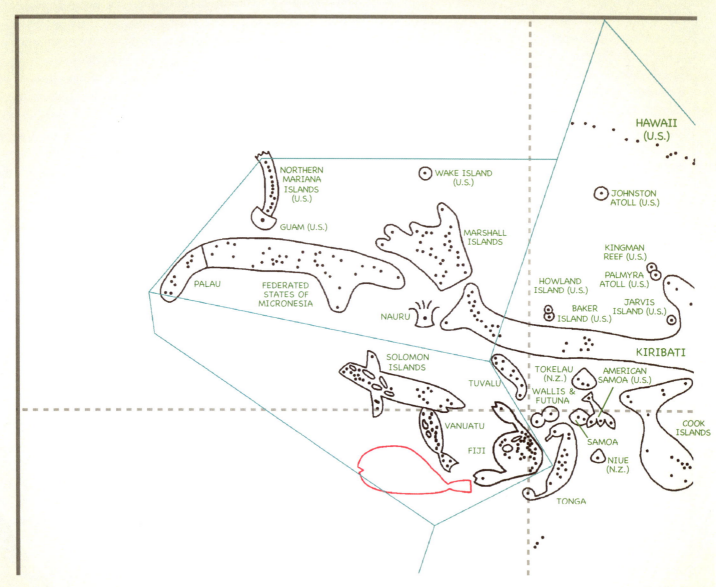

Below the Vanuatuna we will draw the outline of a Sole, which is a type of flatfish not usually found in the South Pacific, but we welcome it on our map as a visitor.

NEW CALEDONIA

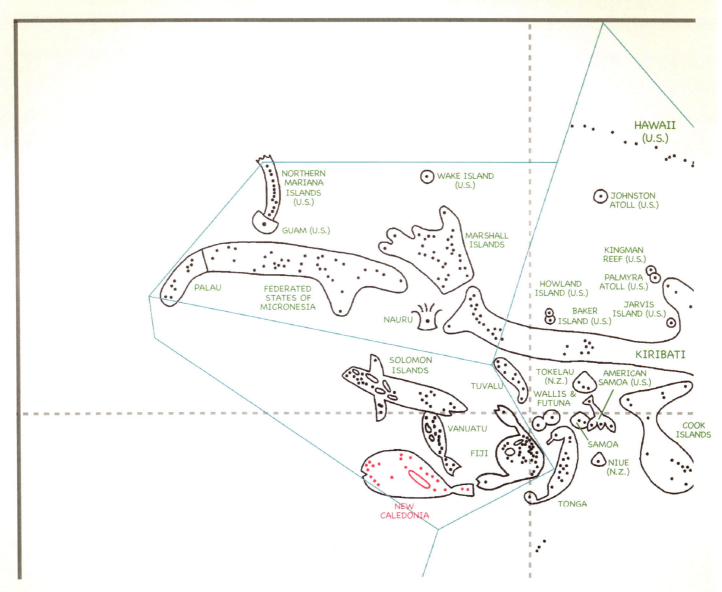

The Sole outlines the French Territory of New Caledonia, which we will rename New Soledonia. This territory consists of one large island called Grande Terre and several smaller islands.

NEW GUINEA

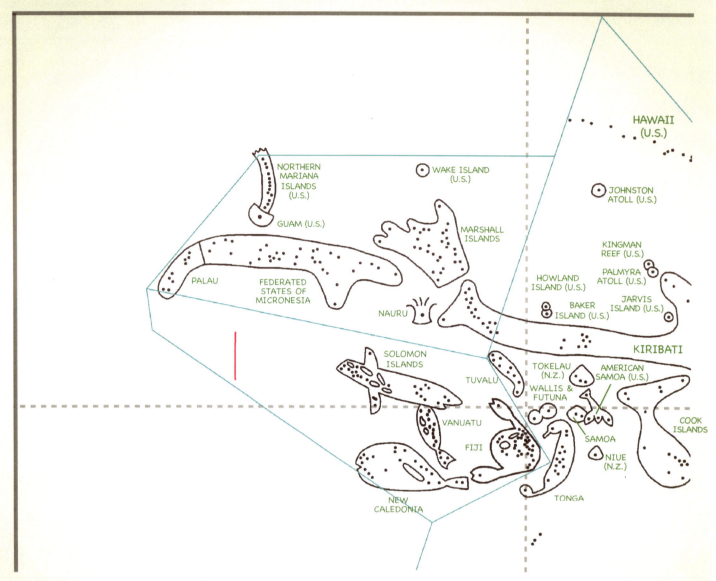

By far the largest island in Melanesia is New Guinea. (In fact it is the second largest island in the world!) New Guinea is divided into two countries: the western half belongs to Indonesia* and the eastern half is the independent country of Papua New Guinea. Begin your drawing with the vertical line that divides the island.

*Although geographically this part of Indonesia belongs in Melanesia, culturally it is most often linked to Asia

NEW GUINEA

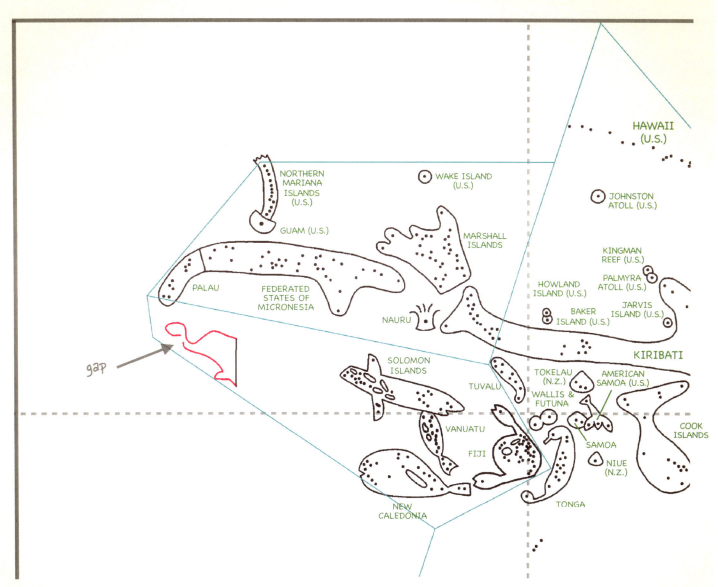

The western half of the island looks like the front end of a dinosaur (which we will call the New Guineasaur). This part of the island contains two of Indonesia's 34 provinces: the dinosaur's neck and head* belong to the province of West Papua and the rest of the front end belongs to the province of Papua. Don't forget to leave a gap in the neck.

*I think the island of New Guinea looks like a dinosaur, but many think it looks like a bird. In fact the "head" is often called the Bird's Head Peninsula.

NEW GUINEA

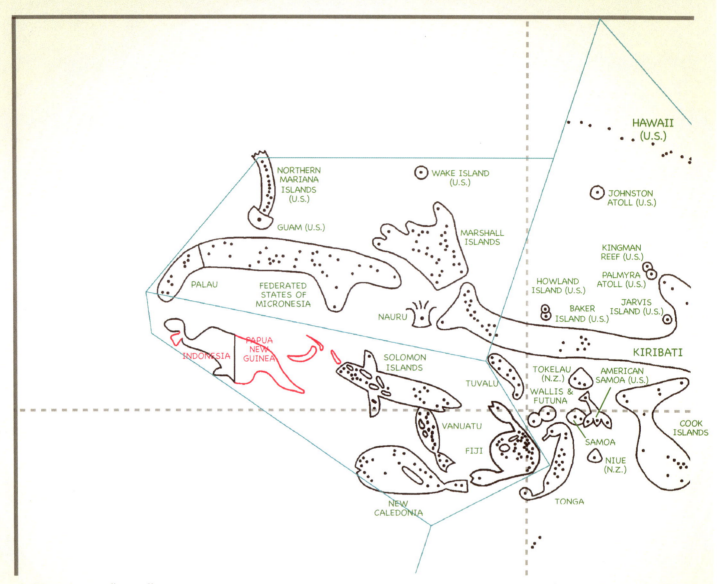

Fill in the "neck" with a little blip that looks like a turkey waddle. The "waddle" is the Bomberai Peninsula. Now draw the eastern half of the island in the shape of a dinosaur's back end with a tail*, then add three islands. This is the country of Papua New Guinea.

*This "tail" is the Papuan Peninsula which is sometimes called the Bird's Tail Peninsula.

NEW GUINEA

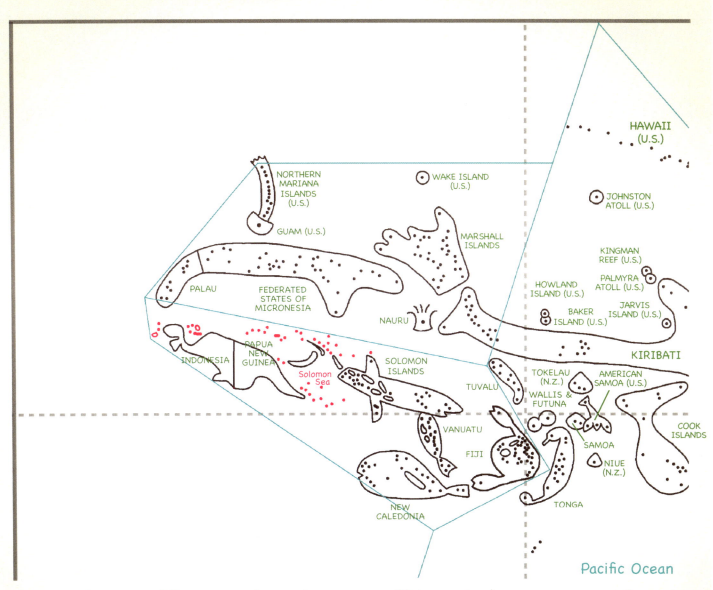

Pacific Ocean

Both Indonesia and Papua New Guinea have many offshore islands. Here are some of them. Also, between the Sharkomon Islands and New Guinea is the Solomon Sea.

AUSTRALIA

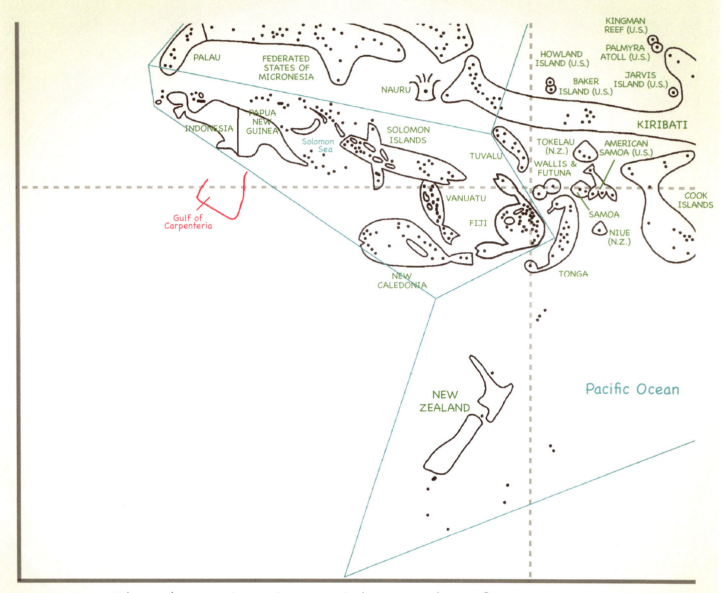

Now we will begin drawing Australia. Directly below the belly of the New Guineasaur draw this hook-like thingy. This is the Gulf of Carpentaria.

AUSTRALIA

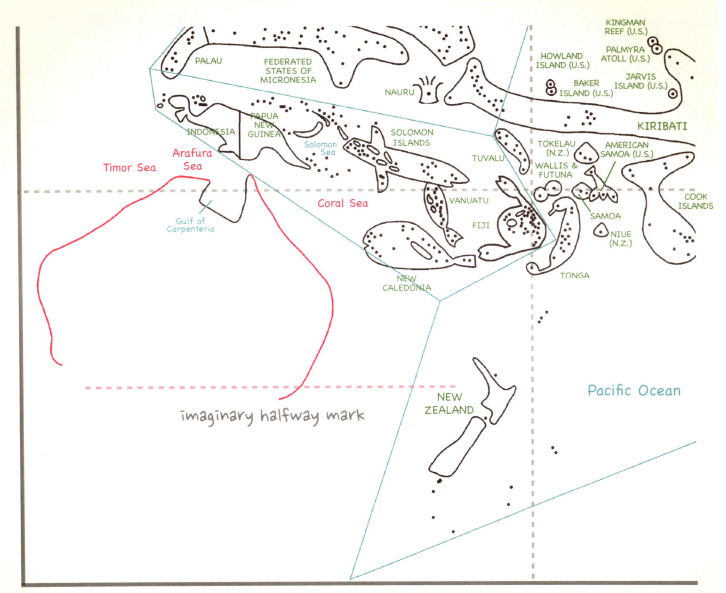

Draw the eastern and western coasts of Australia as shown. Notice that the western coast ends slightly above and the eastern coast ends slightly below the imaginary halfway mark.* Off the northern coast of Australia lie three seas: the Timor Sea, the Arafura Sea and the Coral Sea.

*The imaginary halfway mark divides this quarter of the paper into two horizontal halves.

AUSTRALIA

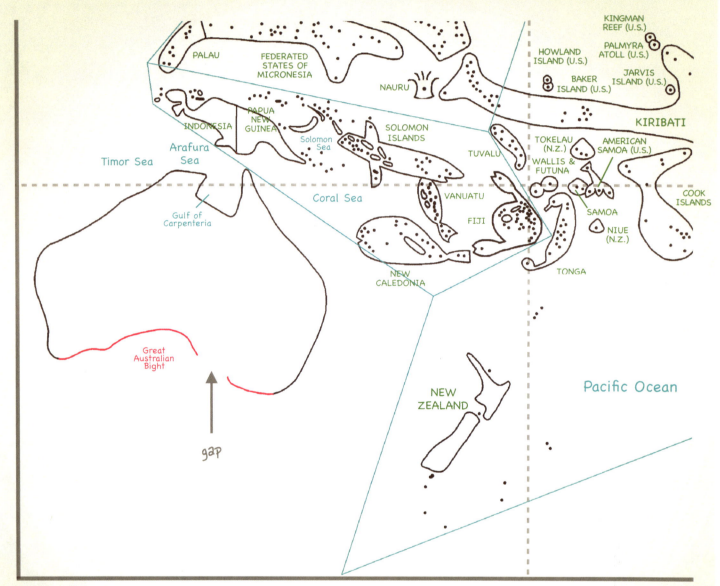

Now draw the southern shore like so. A curve or indent in a shoreline like this is called a "bight." It is as if some giant took a bite out of the coastline, but it is spelled differently. This particular bight is called the Great Australian Bight. Also don't forget to leave a gap in the shoreline.

AUSTRALIA

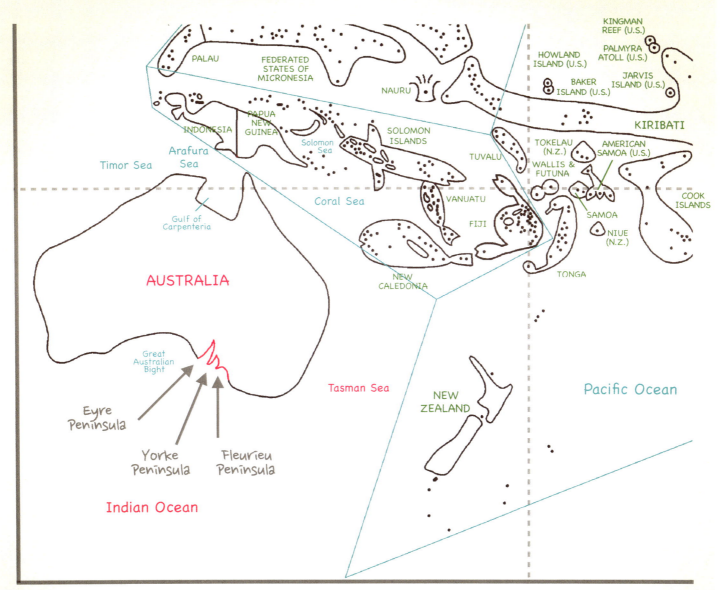

In the gap draw three peninsulas. From west to east they are Eyre, Yorke and Fleurieu Peninsulas. To the west and south of Australia lies the Indian Ocean and to the east between Australia and New Zealand lies the Tasman Sea.

AUSTRALIA

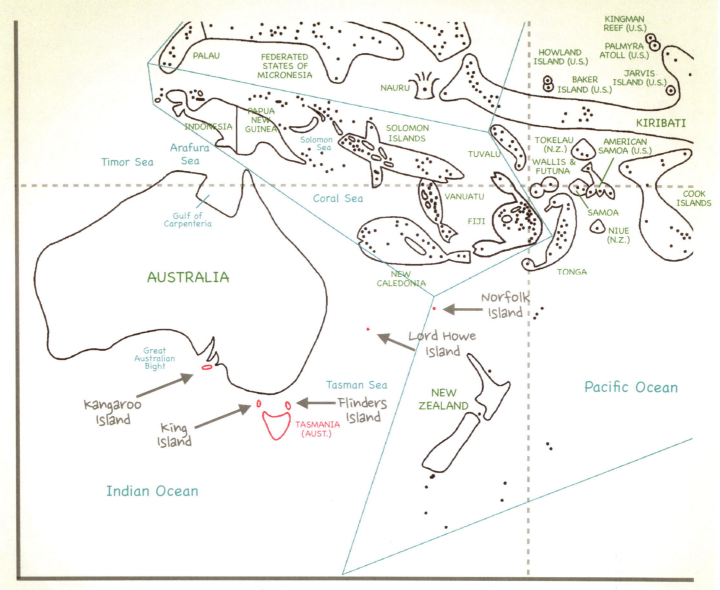

Australia has many, many islands. Below the eastern portion of Australia is the island state of Tasmania. This state includes the large island that bears its name, King Island, Flinders Island and 332 smaller islands which we will not draw. Up in the Great Australian Bight is Kangaroo Island. East of Australia are Norfolk and Lord Howe Islands.

AUSTRALIA

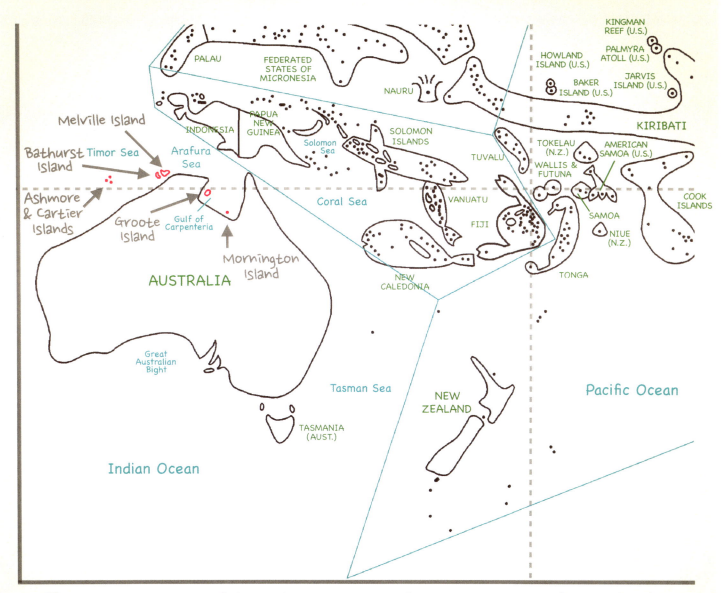

Off the northern shore of Australia in the Timor Sea is a small group of uninhabited islands called the Ashmore and Cartier Islands. East of these, in the Timor Sea are a group of eleven islands called the Tiwi Islands of which Bathurst Island and Melville Island are the largest. In the Gulf of Carpentaria are Groote Island and Mornington Island.

AUSTRALIA

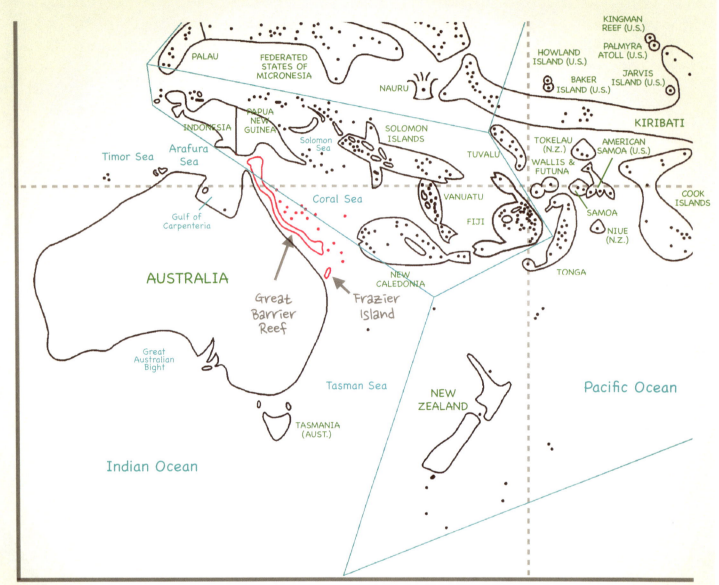

Lastly, we will add three more items: Frazier Island, the Coral Islands (the little dots in the Coral Sea) and the Great Barrier Reef.* The Coral Sea Islands contain over 80 islands (we will draw only seventeen of the largest) all of which are uninhabited except for one that has a very small weather station.

*The Great Barrier Reef contains almost 3,000 individual reefs and 900 islands. This would be way too complicated to draw, so we will outline it instead. It is the thing that looks like a long, skinny tubeworm.

OCEANIA

And that's all, folks!
Congratulations! You can draw Oceania!

Made in the USA
Monee, IL
04 February 2024

52427313R10045